John Rutter

FIVE CHILDHOOD LYRICS

for unaccompanied
mixed voices

MUSIC DEPARTMENT

OXFORD
UNIVERSITY PRESS

This work was given its first performance by the London Concord Singers conducted by Malcolm Cottle on 11 April, 1973, in the Purcell Room, London.

Duration: 9 minutes

for Malcolm Cottle and the London Concord Singers

FIVE CHILDHOOD LYRICS

JOHN RUTTER

1. MONDAY'S CHILD

Words: Traditional

© Oxford University Press 1974

Printed in Great Britain
OXFORD UNIVERSITY PRESS, MUSIC DEPARTMENT, GREAT CLARENDON STREET, OXFORD OX2 6DP

Photocopying this copyright material is ILLEGAL.

18
p espress.
far to go, Fri-day's child is lov-ing and giv-ing,
23
cresc.
3
mf
p
Sa-tur-day's child works hard for his liv-ing, And the child that is born on the
Ah
(hum)
27
mp legato
Sab-bath day Is bon-ny and blithe, and good and gay. Mon-day's
Mon-day's
mf dolce, legato
Mon-day's child

32
child is fair of face, Tues-day's child is full of grace,
child is fair of face, Tues-day's child is full of grace,
is fair of face, Tues-day's child is full of grace,
dim.
37
full of woe, Thurs-day's child has far to
mp legato
cresc.
mf
Wednesday's child is full of woe, Thurs-day's child has far to
p
Wednesday's child is full of woe, Thurs-day's child has far to
41
p dolce, espress.
Fri-day's child is lov-ing and giv-ing,
go, Fri-day's child is lov-ing, and giv-ing,
dim.
go, Fri-day's child is lov-ing and giv-ing,
go, Fri-day's child is lov-ing and giv-ing,

45
cresc.
mp
3
mf
p dolce
Sa-tur-day's child works hard for his liv-ing, And the child that is born on the
Sa-tur-day's child works hard for his liv-ing, And the child that is born on the
Sa-tur-day's child works hard for his liv-ing, And the child that is born on the
Sa-tur-day's child works hard for his liv-ing, And the child that is born on the
49
rall.
slower till the end (♩=c.60)
Sab-bath day Is bon-ny and blithe, and good and gay, is bon-ny and
Sab-bath day Is bon-ny and blithe, and good and gay, is bon-ny and
Sab-bath day Is bon-ny and blithe, and good and gay, is bon-ny and
Sab-bath day Is bon-ny and blithe, and good and gay, is bon-ny and
53
dim.
rall.
a tempo (♩=c.60)
pp
(pp)
blithe, and good and gay. Wednesday's child,
blithe, and good and gay. Tues-day's child,
blithe, and good. Mon-day's child, Tues-day's child, Wednesday's child,
gay.
blithe, and good and gay.

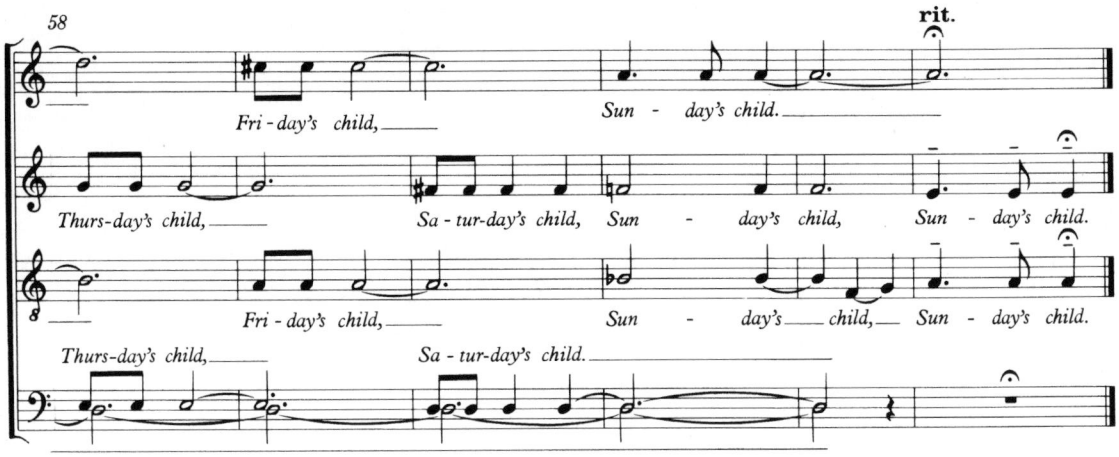

2. THE OWL AND THE PUSSY-CAT

Words by EDWARD LEAR

Fast and light (♩.=120)

SOPRANO
ALTO

TENOR
BASS

mf gaily

The owl and the pus - sy - cat went to sea In a beau - ti - ful pea - green

4 boat, They took some ho - ney, and plen - ty of mo - ney Wrapped up in a five - pound

8 note. The owl looked up to the stars a - bove And sang to a small gui-

mp

p

A.T.B. *Ah*

p

12
tar,
dim.
Ah
p cresc.
mf dim.
Ah
mp
A. Ah
Ah
T. 'O love - ly pus - sy! O pus - sy, my love, What a beau - ti - ful pus - sy you
mp cresc.
mf
mp
dim.
p cresc.
mf dim.
mp
Ah
Ah
16
Ah
Ah
you are, you are, you are, Ah
are, you are, you are! What a beau - -
20
rall.
a tempo
Pus - sy said to the owl, 'You
mp
p
a beau - ti - ful pus - sy you are!' Ah
- ti - ful pus - sy you are!' Ah
a beau - ti - ful pus - sy you are!'
p Ah
24
e - le - gant fowl! How charm - ing - ly sweet you sing! O let us be mar - ried! too
Ah
Ah

28
long we have tar - ried: But what shall we do for a ring?'
mf
They sailed a - way for a
Ah
Ah
mf

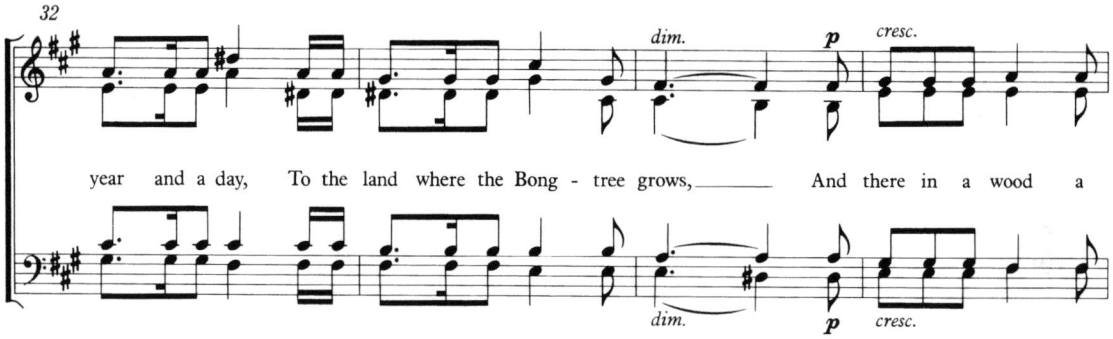
32
dim.
p
cresc.
year and a day, To the land where the Bong - tree grows, And there in a wood a
dim.
p
cresc.

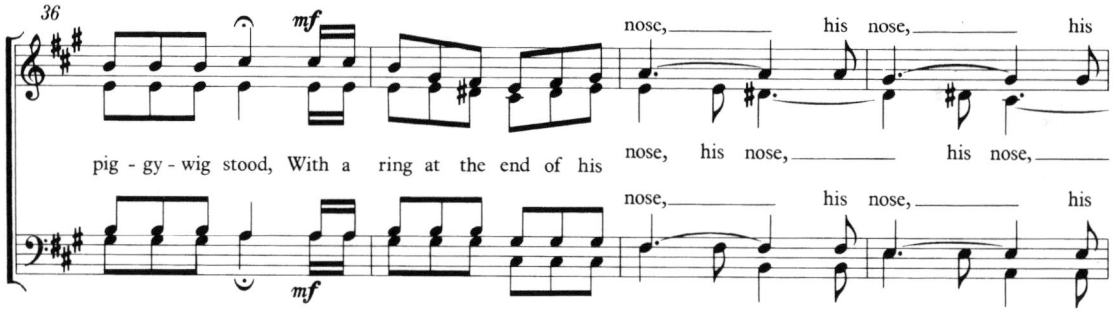
36
mf
nose, his nose, his
pig - gy - wig stood, With a ring at the end of his nose, his nose, his nose,
nose, his nose, his
mf
nose, his nose, his nose, his nose, his

40
nose, with a ring at the end of his nose.
rall.
his nose, with a ring at the end of his nose, with a ring at the
nose, with a ring
nose, with a ring at the end of his nose.

44
a tempo
f
end of his nose.
Ah
f T. and B. unis.
'Dear pig, are you wil - ling to sell for one shil - ling Your ring?' Said the pig - gy 'I
48
Ah
will.' So they took it a - way and were mar - ried next day By the tur - key who lives on the
52
mf
Ah
mf
hill. They dined on mince, and sli - ces of quince, Which they ate with a run - ci - ble
56
dim.
lightly
pp
And hand in hand, on the edge of the sand, They
spoon, And
pp
dim.
spoon, And hand in hand, on the edge of the sand,
*easier alternative

59
S.
danced, they danced, they danced, they danced, they danced, they danced, they
cresc.
mp
A.
danced, they danced, they danced, they danced, they danced, they danced, they
T.
danced by the light of the moon, they danced by the light of the moon, they
B.
pp
They danced by the light of the moon, they danced by the light of the
63
danced, they danced, they danced by the light of the
danced, they danced, they danced by the light of the moon,
danced by the light of the moon, they danced,
moon, by the light of the moon,
67
moon, they danced, they danced, they danced, they danced, they
they danced, they danced, they danced, they danced, they
f
by the light of the moon, they danced, they
mf
they danced, they danced, they

71
cresc.
ff
danced, they danced, they danced by the light of the moon, by the
danced, they danced, they danced by the light of the moon, by the
danced, they danced, they danced by the light of the moon, by the
danced, they danced, they danced by the light of the moon, by the
75
light of the moon, by the light of the moon,
light of the moon, by the light of the moon,
light of the moon, the moon, the moon, the
light of the moon, the moon, the moon, the
79
allargando
by the light of the moon, by the light of the moon.
by the light of the moon, by the light of the moon.
moon, the moon, by the light of the moon.
moon, the moon, by the light of the moon.

3. WINDY NIGHTS

Words by R.L.STEVENSON*

*from *A Child's Garden of Verses*

7
cresc.
mf
-e - ver the wind is high, All night long in the
cresc.
mf
-e - ver the wind is high, All night long in the
cresc.
p
Gal - lop and gal - lop and gal - lop, gal - lop, gal - lop a - bout,
p
- bout, gal - lop, gal - lop, gal - lop a -
cresc.
p
- bout, gal - lop and gal - lop, gal - lop, gal - lop a - bout, gal - lop and
cresc.
p
gal - lop, gal - lop, gal - lop, gal - lop, gal - lop, gal - lop, gal - lop, gal - lop,
10
cresc.
f
dark and wet, A man goes rid - ing
cresc.
f
dark and wet, A man goes rid - ing
mf
gal - lop, gal - lop, gal - lop a - bout, gal - lop, gal - lop,
cresc.
mf
- bout, gal - lop, gal - lop, gal - lop and gal - lop a - bout,
cresc.
mf
gal - lop, gal - lop, gal - lop a - bout, gal - lop and gal - lop and gal - lop, gal - lop,
cresc.
mf
gal - lop, gal - lop, gal - lop, gal - lop, gal - lop, gal - lop, gal - lop, gal - lop, gal - lop,

13
S.1
by.
mp
dim.
Gal - lop and gal - lop and
S.2
by.
A.1
by.
Gal - lop and gal - lop and
A.2
by.
Gal - lop, gal - lop,
T.
gal - lop and gal - lop and gal - lop, gal - lop, gal - lop a - bout,
B.1
gal - lop and gal - lop a - bout, gal - lop a - bout,
B.2
gal - lop, gal - lop, gal - lop, gal - lop, gal - lop a - bout,
16
pp
gal - lop, gal - lop, gal - lop a - bout,
Gal - lop and gal - lop and gal - lop, gal - lop, gal - lop a -
gal - lop, gal - lop, gal - lop a - bout,
gal - lop, gal - lop, gal - lop, gal - lop and gal - lop and gal - lop, gal - lop, gal - lop a -
p legato
Late in the night when the fires are out,
Late in the night when the fires are out,

19
cresc.
p
S.1
Gal - lop, gal - lop, gal - lop a - bout,
S.2
- bout,
Gal - lop and gal - lop and gal - lop, gal - lop a -
A.1
Gal - lop, gal - lop, gal - lop a - bout,
A.2
- bout,
Gal - lop and gal - lop and gal - lop, gal - lop a -
T.
mp
Why does he gal - lop and gal - lop a -
B.
Why does he gal - lop and gal - lop a -
22
mp cresc. molto
ff
Gal - lop and gal - lop and gal - lop, gal - lop, gal - lop,
Gal - lop and gal - lop and
- bout,
gal - lop, gal - lop, gal - lop a - bout,
gal - lop and
mf
- bout?
B.1
B.2
Gal - lop, gal - lop,

25
S.
A.
T.
B.1
B.2
dim.
f
gal - lop, gal - lop, gal - lop a - bout.
When -
gal - lop, gal - lop, gal - lop and gal - lop and gal - lop a - bout.
gal - lop, gal - lop, gal - lop and gal - lop and gal - lop and gal - lop, gal - lop, gal - lop.
gal - lop, gal - lop, gal - lop, gal - lop, gal - lop, gal - lop, gal - lop, gal - lop.
28
- e - ver the trees are cry - ing a - loud, And ships are tossed at
B.
31
mf
cresc.
sea, By, on the high - way, low and loud,

36
f
dim.
mp
By at the gal - lop goes he.
By at the gal - lop goes he.
f
mp dim.
Gal - lop and gal - lop and gal - lop, gal - lop, gal - lop a -
Gal - lop, gal - lop, gal - lop, gal - lop, gal - lop a -
39
p cresc.
By at the gal - lop he goes, and then
By he comes back at the
By at the gal - lop he goes, and
By he comes back at the
pp cresc.
- bout,
and
By, by he comes
- bout,
By
42
S.
gal - lop a - gain.
A.
gal - lop a - gain.
T.
back at the gal - lop a - gain.
B.1
pp cresc. poco a poco
Gal - lop and gal - lop and gal - lop, gal - lop, gal - lop and
B.2
Gal - lop, gal - lop, gal - lop, gal - lop, gal - lop,

45
S.
A.
T.1
T.2
B.1
B.2
mp cresc. poco a poco
Gal - lop and gal - lop and
p cresc. poco a poco
mp cresc.
Gal - lop and gal - lop and gal - lop, gal - lop, gal - lop a - bout, Gal - lop and
gal - lop and gal - lop and gal - lop, gal - lop, gal - lop a - bout, Gal - lop and
gal - lop, gal - lop, gal - lop, gal - lop, gal - lop, gal - lop, gal - lop,
48
(senza rall.)
f cresc.
ff
Gal - lop and gal - lop and gal - lop.
mf cresc.
Gal - lop and gal - lop and gal - lop and gal - lop and gal - lop.
gal - lop, gal - lop, gal - lop a - bout, gal - lop and gal - lop and gal - lop and gal - lop.
gal - lop, gal - lop, gal - lop, gal - lop, gal - lop and gal - lop and gal - lop.

4. MATTHEW, MARK, LUKE AND JOHN

Words: Traditional

Poco più mosso (♩= c.96)
I lie on. Four cor - ners to my
23 (Hum)
bed, Four an - gels round my
28
32
head;
S.
(pp)
One to watch, and one
p
A.
(pp)
And one to
p
pp
T.
p
One to watch, and one
dim. pp
B.
(pp)
And one to

36 rall. meno mosso (♩ = c.80) pp legato e dolce attacca No. 5

And two to bear my soul a - way.

pp attacca No. 5

to pray.

pray, to pray.

to pray, to pray.

pray, to pray.

5. SING A SONG OF SIXPENCE

Words and melody: Traditional

Very fast and light (♩ = c.184)

SOPRANO

ALTO pp

Sing a song of six - pence, sing a song

TENOR pp

Sing a song of six - pence, sing a song

BASS pp

Sing a song of six - pence, sing a song

7
pp
Sing a song of six - pence, A poc-ket full of rye;
of six - pence, sing a song of six - pence,
of six - pence, sing a song of six - pence,
of six - pence, sing a song of six - pence,
13
Four and twen-ty black - birds, Baked in a pie. When the pie was o - pened The
sing a song of six - pence, sing a song
sing a song of six - pence, sing a song
sing a song of six - pence, sing a song
19
cresc.
mp
dim.
birds be - gan to sing; Was not that a dain - ty dish To set be - fore the king?
of six - pence, sing a song of six - pence,
of six - pence, sing a song of six - pence,
of six - pence, sing a song of six - pence,

25
sing.
f subito
> dim.
sing a song of six - pence, sing a song
f subito
> dim.
sing a song of six - pence, sing a song
31
f >
Sing a song of six - pence, A poc - ket full of rye;
f >
Sing a song of six - pence, A poc - ket full of rye;
mf >
of six - pence, sing a song of six - pence,
mf >
of six - pence, sing a song of six - pence,
37
Four and twen - ty black - birds Baked in a pie. When the pie was o - pened The
Four and twen - ty black - birds Baked in a pie. When the pie was o - pened The
sing a song of six - pence, sing a song
sing a song of six - pence, sing a song

43
birds be - gan to sing; Was not that a dain - ty dish To set be - fore the king?
birds be - gan to sing; Was not that a dain - ty dish To set be - fore the king?
of six - pence, sing a song of six - pence,
of six - pence, sing a song of six - pence,
49 (f)
Sing a song of six - pence, sing a song
(f)
Sing a song of six - pence, sing a song
sing.
sing.
55 dim.
mf
of six - pence, sing a song of six - pence,
dim.
mf
of six - pence, sing a song of six - pence,
mf
The
f
mf
The king was in his count - ing house, Count - ing out his mo - ney; The

61
sing a song of six - pence, sing a song
sing a song of six - pence, sing a song
queen was in the par - lour, Eat - ing bread and ho - ney.
cresc.
queen was in the par - lour, Eat - ing bread and ho - ney.
The maid was in the gar - den,
67
cresc.
of six - pence, sing a song of six - pence,
cresc.
of six - pence, sing a song of six - pence,
f
There came a lit - tle black - bird And snapp'd off her nose.
f
Hang - ing out the clothes,
There came a lit - tle black - bird And snapp'd off her nose.
73 ff dim.
mf
sing a song of six - pence, sing.
ff dim.
mf
sing a song of six - pence, sing.
ff dim.
mf dim.
Sing a song of six - pence, sing a song
ff dim.
mf dim.
Sing a song of six - pence, sing a song

79
p
Sing a song of six - pence, A poc-ket full of rye;
p
Ah
p
of six - pence, sing. Sing a song of six - pence, A poc-ket full of
p
of six - pence, sing.
85
cresc.
Four and twen-ty black - birds, Baked in a pie. When the pie was o - pened The
cresc.
Ah
The
cresc.
rye; Four and twen-ty black - birds, Baked in a pie. When the pie was
cresc.
Ah
Ah
91
mf
birds be-gan to sing; Was not that a dain-ty dish To set be-fore the king?
mf
birds be-gan to sing; Was not that a dain-ty dish To set be-fore the king?
mf
o - pened The birds be-gan to sing; Was not that a dain-ty dish To set be-fore the
mf
Was not that a dain-ty dish To set be-fore the king?

97
Sing a song of six - pence, A poc - ket full of
Sing a song of six - pence, A poc-ket full of rye; Four and twen-ty black - birds
king? Sing a song of six - pence, A poc-ket full of rye; Four and twen-ty black -
Sing a song of six - pence, A poc - ket
103
rye; Four and twen - ty black - birds
baked in a pie, Four and twen-ty black - - birds. When the pie was
-birds, Four and twen - ty black - birds.
full of rye; Four and twen - ty black - birds.
109
Baked in a pie. When the pie was
o - pened The birds be-gan to sing; Sing a song of six - pence, A
Four and twen - ty black - - birds, Sing a song of
Sing a

115
ff
o - pened The birds be - gan to sing;
ff
poc - ket full of rye; When the pie was o - pened,
ff
six - pence, A poc - ket full of rye;
ff
song of six - - pence,
121
pp subito
Was not that a dain - ty dish To set be - fore the king?
pp subito
f
Was not that a dain - ty dish? Sing a song
pp subito
f
Was not that a dain - ty dish? Sing a song
pp subito
f
Was not that a dain - ty dish? Sing a song
127
dim. molto
of six - pence, sing a song of six - pence,
dim. molto
of six - pence, sing a song of six - pence,
dim. molto
of six - pence, sing a song of six - pence,

Reproduced and printed by
Halstan & Co. Ltd., Amersham, Bucks., England

Produced by J. P. Homer
OXFORD UNIVERSITY PRESS